CREATING A BUDGET

Gillian Houghton

PowerKiDS press

New York

Published in 2009 by The Rosen Publishing Group, Inc.
29 East 21st Street, New York, NY 10010

Copyright © 2009 by The Rosen Publishing Group, Inc.

All rights reserved. No part of this book may be reproduced in any form without permission in writing from the publisher, except by a reviewer.

First Edition

Editor: Joanne Randolph
Book Design: Julio Gil
Photo Researcher: Jessica Gerweck

Photo Credits: Cover, back cover, pp. 13, 14 Shutterstock.com; p. 5 © Purestock/Getty Images; p. 6 © STOCK4B/Getty Images; p. 9 © Peter Cade/Getty Images; p. 10 © Jeremy Hoare/Age Fotostock; p. 17 © Erik Dreyer/Getty Images; p. 18 © Mel Yates/Getty Images; p. 21 © Johner/Getty Images.

Library of Congress Cataloging-in-Publication Data

Houghton, Gillian.
 Creating a budget / Gillian Houghton. — 1st ed.
    p. cm. — (Invest kids)
 Includes index.
 ISBN 978-1-4358-2774-5 (library binding) — ISBN 978-1-4358-3209-1 (pbk.)
 ISBN 978-1-4358-3215-2 (6-pack)
  1. Budgets, Personal—Juvenile literature. 2. Finance, Personal—Juvenile literature. I. Title.
HG179.H613 2009
332.024—dc22
                                             2008039977

Manufactured in the United States of America

Contents

The Plan	4
Your Budget	7
Know Your Goal	8
Know Your Habits	11
Get a Job	12
Earning Money	15
Write It Down	16
Keeping It Safe	19
What Are Your Expenses?	20
Spending Wisely	22
Glossary	23
Index	24
Web Sites	24

The Plan

You see it in the window. It is a shiny, green bicycle. It looks like it could go very fast. You want it!

Then you see the price tag, which tells you how much the bicycle costs. Do you have enough money? If not, how can you **earn** the money you need? If you save enough money and spend it on the bicycle, will you have enough left over to buy the other things that you need and want?

Questions like these will help you make a plan for how to save and spend your money. This plan is called a **budget**.

This girl is shopping for a bicycle. Once she finds the one she likes and knows how much it costs, she can make a budget and get started on saving to buy it.

You can start your budget with the money you have in your piggy bank. Add up how much you have saved, then keep track of what you put in and what you take out.

Your Budget

A budget is a plan for earning, saving, and spending money. We earn money by working. We save money by putting it away somewhere. The best place to save your money is in an **account** at the bank. We spend money on things we need and on things we want. We need things such as a place to live and food to eat. We want things such as toys and candy.

It is important to keep track of how much you earn, save, and spend. If you spend all of your money on the things you want, you will not be able to **afford** the things you need.

Know Your Goal

A budget can help you reach your goals. A goal is something you decide to work toward. Let's say that it is your goal to buy that green bicycle you saw in the window.

What do you know about your goal? The price tag says that the shiny, green bicycle costs $75. You empty your piggy bank and count every penny. You have $15. That means you will need to save $60 before you can afford the bicycle. That may seem like a lot of money, but do not give up. If you make a plan of how you will earn money and start saving, you will find that those dollars add up quickly.

You can keep track of your money with a piece of paper, a pencil, and a calculator if you have one. Write your goal at the top to help you remember what you are saving for.

Maybe you spend money every week on ice cream. If you want to save your money for something else, you will need to buy less ice cream to reach your goal quickly.

Know Your Habits

What are your spending **habits**? Where does all of your money go? Habits are things we do again and again, often without thinking about what we are doing. To find out what your spending habits are, make a list of every cent you spend for a month. At the end of the month, look over your list.

Did you spend money on things that you could do without? If you want to reach your goal quickly, you may need to break some of your spending habits. Make a few rules for how you could do this and how much money you will spend each month.

Get a Job

Most people earn money by doing work for someone. Some people earn money by selling goods, or things. Other people sell services, or the work that they do.

How can you earn money around your house or around your neighborhood? Ask the people in your family if there are chores, or little jobs, that you can do around the house. Ask the people who live near you if they have work for you to do. Think about what you are good at and what kind of work you would enjoy. Would you like walking your neighbor's dog, clearing the snow, or cutting grass?

There are lots of ways to make money as long as you do not mind working hard. This girl is raking leaves to earn money.

These boys charge their neighbors $10 to wash their cars, and they plan to wash five cars in a week. They will earn about $50, or $25 each, by the end of the week.

Earning Money

When someone gives you a job, he agrees to pay you a certain amount of money in return for the good or service you give him. Every time you are paid, make a note of it. **Calculate** how much you can plan to earn every month.

For example, your neighbor asks you to cut the grass on her lawn one time each week, or four times each month. Your neighbor agrees to pay you $5 every time you cut the grass. That means your neighbor will pay you $20 every month. Knowing how much money you are likely to make in a month will help you plan your budget.

Write It Down

A budget works best when it is written down. You want to be sure you are keeping track of everything you earn, save, and spend. Make a list of how much you plan to earn, save, and spend each month. If your neighbor pays you $20 every month, and you spend $10 every month on candy and toys, you will be able to save $10 each month.

At that rate, it will take you six months to save enough money to buy the bicycle. What if you want the bicycle in three months, though? How much do you need to save each month in order to reach this goal?

This boy makes money selling movie tickets, and this girl is spending hers to buy the tickets. They both should write down what they earn and spend in their budgets.

This boy shows off his savings during a visit to the toy store. Saving your money lets you buy things that you need and things that you want.

Keeping It Safe

It is important to put the money you earn in a safe place. You may decide to keep your money in a piggy bank or in a shoe box under your bed. It would be even better if you kept your money in a savings account at the bank. If you keep your money in a savings account, it will be safe and it will grow.

When you put your money in a savings account, the bank pays you **interest**, or extra money. The longer you keep your money in the bank, the more interest you earn. Interest will help you reach your goal even sooner!

What Are Your Expenses?

Even while you save money, you may need or want to spend some money along the way. You may need to spend money on a can of gas for your lawn mower. You may want to go to a movie after mowing the neighbor's lawn. The can of gas and the movie are **expenses**, or goods and services you spend money on.

Every time you spend money, make a note of it. **Subtract** the amount you spend from the amount you have earned. Remember, every time you spend your money, you are that much farther from reaching your goal.

This boy plans to open a lemonade stand and sell homemade lemonade. To make lemonade, he had to buy lemons and sugar, which were his expenses.

Spending Wisely

Spend your money carefully. Think about what is really important to you. Ask yourself whether going to the movie is worth it, because then it will take a little longer before you can afford the bicycle.

It is also important to be a smart shopper. Will the price of the bicycle be discounted, or lowered, at the end of the summer? Sellers sometimes lower prices in order to sell their goods quickly. Often, prices are discounted at the end of a season, when people are less likely to be shopping for a certain thing. That's a good time to buy! Be a smart **consumer** and make the most out of your money.

GLOSSARY

account (uh-KOWNT) A special place where a bank keeps money set aside for a person.

afford (uh-FORD) To have enough money to pay for something.

budget (BUH-jit) A plan for spending that keeps track of the money that comes in and the money that is spent.

calculate (KAL-kyuh-layt) To figure out using math.

consumer (kun-SOO-mer) A person who buys goods and services.

earn (ERN) To be paid money for work.

expenses (ik-SPENS-iz) The goods and services on which a person spends money.

habits (HA-bits) The usual, or common, ways a person does something.

interest (IN-ter-est) The extra cost that someone pays in order to borrow money. Banks pay money to people with savings accounts for letting the bank borrow that money.

subtract (sub-TRAKT) To take away.

INDEX

A
account, 7, 19
amount, 15, 20

B
bank, 7–8, 19
bicycle, 4, 8, 16, 22

C
cent, 11
consumer, 22

F
family, 12
food, 7

G
goal(s), 8, 11, 16, 19–20
good(s), 12, 15, 22

I
interest, 19

J
job(s), 12, 15

L
list, 11, 16

P
penny, 8

plan, 4, 7–8
price tag, 4, 8

Q
questions, 4

S
service(s), 12, 15

T
toys, 7, 16

W
work, 12

WEB SITES

Due to the changing nature of Internet links, PowerKids Press has developed an online list of Web sites related to the subject of this book. This site is updated regularly. Please use this link to access the list:
www.powerkidslinks.com/ikids/budget/